An Essential Photog

Lancaster

Mark Pickup

and

Andrew McQueen

THIS BOOK IS A PUBLICATION OF
McQueen Publishing

4 Johnson Close
Abraham Heights
LANCASTER
LA1 5EU
United Kingdom

First Edition October 2013

Conditions of Sale

Great efforts have been made by the Publisher and Author to
ensure that the information contained in this book is accurate.
Information can become out of date, however, and errors can be
made. This book is sold, therefore, on the condition that neither
the Publisher nor the Author can be held legally responsible for
the consequences of any error or omission there may be.

ISBN 978-0-9573374-4-2

Printed by Berforts Information Press

CONTENTS

1

Lancaster Castle

There has been a defensive building on the site of Lancaster castle for thousands of years and the modern day castle reflects this rich and varied history. The site of the castle is on the summit of a small hill overlooking the River Lune which is only 320 metres away. It is in a commanding strategic position dominating the river and the surrounding area reflecting the roman grasp of military defence in hostile country.

The Romans

The first roman fort on this site would have been built

Lancaster Castle

by Julius Agricola: a roman general, consul, and governor of Britannia in AD 77. He is largely responsible for the final roman conquest and pacification of Britannia. It was his troops which built many of the first forts and roads throughout the North of England consolidating the roman hold over Britannia. The first roman fort at Lancaster was built in around AD 80 by roman legionaries and some of the later roman building materials have been incorporated by medieval masons into the fabric of the castle.

The Anglo Saxons

Little is known of Lancaster from the end of the roman occupation until the Norman Conquest of 1066. During this period Lancaster was for a time the saxon capital of southern Cumbria. It is thought that there existed a saxon fort on the castle site, which incorporated the older roman defences. The saxon fort would likely have been a wooden construction with palisades rather than a stone built castle which came later under the Norman Conquest.

The Norman Conquest

Lancaster castle's first masonry defences were begun in the 12th Century after the Norman Conquest. Lancaster is recorded in the Doomsday Book of 1086 as 'Loncastre', and was then only a part of Halton Crown Manor. Halton is a few miles up stream of the River Lune from Lancaster.

Halton Crown Manor including Loncastre was given by William the Conqueror to Roger De Poitou as a reward for leading the right wing of William's army at the Battle of Hastings. As the normans were invaders in a hostile territory, much like the romans, Roger De Poitou took Loncastre as his residence, the existing saxon defensive buildings providing an ideal defensive site.

Lancaster Castle

The Lungess Tower

The keep within Lancaster castle was the first substantial building on the site to have been built from masonry. The building was probably begun by Roger De Poitou as early as the 12th Century although it could have been added to and improved at a later date. It is a remarkable example of a norman keep called the Lungess Tower.

The keep rises to an imposing height of almost eighty feet. It is a formidable construction with walls that are in places ten feet thick. The original entrance to this keep would have been by a flight of steps leading up to the first floor, reflecting its defensive nature. Surmounting this impressive keep is a later tower known as John O'Gaunt's Chair. This is an embattled turret rising ten feet above the original parapet and was probably added during the 1400s.

The John O'Gaunt Gatehouse

The impressive twin towered John O'Gaunt gatehouse is the finest and most impressive of its date and type in the country. Although named after his father it was first built by John O'Gaunt's son, Henry IV, the tenth King of England after he had deposed Richard II. Henry IV spent much of his reign defending himself against rebellion.

Today, the crenellated battlements of the gatehouse soar more than sixty feet above its enormous sloping plinths. It

has two massive semi-octagonal turrets and its battlements are built over corbels which allow them to overhang the main wall of the gatehouse giving defenders an ideal position to defend against any attack on the formidable gates.

The entrance is over sixty feet deep with walls that are a staggering ten feet thick. The loopholes in each tower allowed archers to fire on attackers from the guardrooms behind and can still be seen, although they would have originally been of cruciform shape. Even today standing at its open gateway it can easily be imagined how impregnable the gatehouse would have been. With its portcullis down and huge oak gates closed it would have been a formidable task to breach this gatehouse.

Like much of Lancaster castle the gatehouse has been constantly added to and updated over the centuries. For example, the statue in the niche above the main archway is that of John O'Gaunt. This is a much later 19th Century addition and did not feature on the original gatehouse.

Lancaster Castle

The Witches Tower

The Well Tower, sometimes called the Witches Tower, lies to the north of the gatehouse. The name Well Tower is taken from the fact that there is a deep well hidden within its walls. It is thought to date from the 14th century. The basement of this tower was converted during the early part of the 17th century into a dungeon and is thought to have been used to hold the Lancashire Witches.

These women were held here in their misery while they awaited their trial in 1612. Ten of these women were ultimately found guilty of witchcraft. They were sentenced to death and taken to nearby Lancaster Moor were they were executed by hanging.

For much of its life Lancaster castle was the centre of justice for the whole of Lancashire. Many offences were punishable by death and these were duly carried out at the castle or at Lancaster Moor.

Much of the castle was substantially modified during the 18th Century and since then it has mainly been used as a court and a prison. During this rebuilding and modification much of the medieval curtain wall and several ancient towers were removed.

Although Lancaster Crown Court still sits in part of the castle much of it is open to the public and the castle offers guided tours.

2

The Judges Lodgings

The Judges Lodgings occupy the site of the medieval home of Sir Robert De Holland built in around 1322. He was considered a traitor by the Lancastrian rebels after he defected to King Edward II at the battle of Boroughbridge and was subsequently beheaded.

The site lies on Church Street which is one of the oldest streets in Lancaster and it was on this street that the most important and influential people lived in medieval times.

The current house or Judges Lodgings was built in the 1630s by the then Keeper of the Castle, Thomas Covell and it is Lancaster's oldest existing town house. Thomas Covell is

possibly more famously known as Lancaster's witch hunter and it was he who presided over the Pendle Witch Trials, imprisoning and executing these women. He died aged 78 and is buried in the chancel at the Priory Church of St Mary's next to Lancaster castle. Later the house was mainly used as lodgings for the visiting judges attending the Assizes court at Lancaster castle.

Much like the castle the house has undergone centuries of alterations and additions. It is built of Lancaster freestone, a light coloured sandstone, perhaps taken from the quarries now occupied by Williamson Park. It incorporates elements probably taken from earlier building some of which, such as the fireplace, have survived since the 1550s. The house is now a thriving museum with a fine collection of rare Gillow furniture and the Museum of Childhood.

The cross which stands outside the house is called the Covell Cross but it was in fact erected to commemorate the coronation of King Edward VII in 1902. A more ancient cross is known originally to have stood in this place.

13

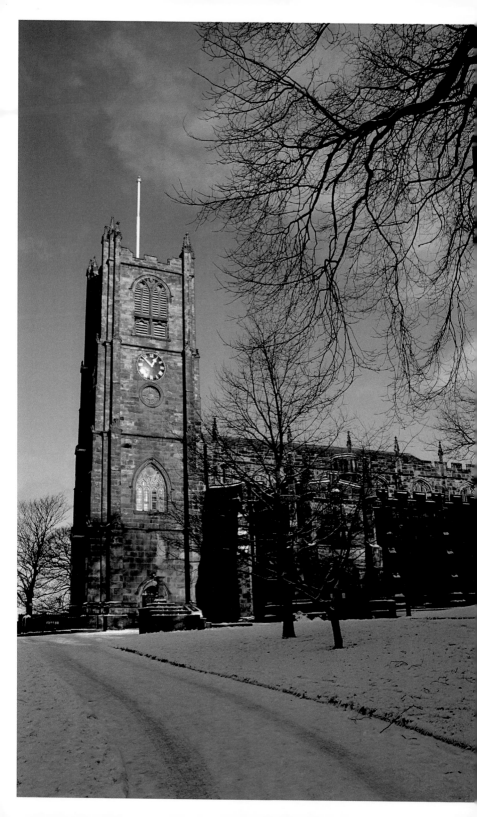

3

The Priory Church
of St Mary

The Priory Church of St Mary has in one form or another occupied its present site since at least the 9th Century and it may be possible that a religious building has existed here as far back as the 6th Century. So although the Church looks to belong to the castle it is likely to have existed before the more modern castle was built.

There is much evidence for the early date of the original priory not least of which are the many Anglo Saxon coins and a small hoard which have been found nearby indicating the existence of a monastery. There is also much Anglo Saxon masonry incorporated into some of the walls of the later

building.

After the Norman Conquest, Roger De Poitou gave the church to the Norman Abbey of Seez. Such gifted alien priories were usually used by the Normans as rent gathering centres and this was the case with Lancaster Priory. It generated a revenue of 50 marks which was sent to the Abbey in France.

This is something that rankled later English kings as they watched money flow to the then hostile French. Henry V dissolved these foreign owned priories in 1414 and St Mary's Priory was given to his newly founded nunnery of Syon in Middlesex. In 1430 the church became a parish church and remains so to this day.

The magnificent church we see today is mainly the result of the massive rebuilding programme of the 15th Century. The majority of the building is constructed from great blocks of sandstone which is readily evident in its outer walls. These contrast sharply with some of the older parts of the priory which are built of early rubble walling thought to date from the Norman period.

One of the great features of this church are the beautiful medieval choir stalls dating from the 1300s. They have been much moved around over the centuries and it is remarkable that they have survived at all. The marvellous needlework panels were made by local women.

There has been much conjecture as to the original location of these stalls and whether they came from another abbey such as nearby Cockersand Abbey, but there is no reason they could not have been originally made for Lancaster.

The bell tower today is a latter rebuilding of the original tower which would have stood apart from the church, separated from it by a charnel house – where stray bones found in new grave excavations were stored. In 1743 a new peal of bells was bought for the priory from Abel Rudall of Gloucester. The original tower was raised by some 10-15 feet so that the sound of the bells would travel further. Unfortunately, the old could not carry the new and soon after completion the bell tower began to collapse. This tower was torn down and rebuilt in its current location in 1756.

The bells that ring out today were paid for by millionaire philanthropist, Lord Ashton in response to a request made by the vicar to his congregation which was probably instigated by the installation of new bells in St Peter's Roman Catholic Cathedral. Not to be outdone, James Williamson duly obliged and he donated the £1000 needed to pay for a peel of eight bells made by Taylors of Loughborough. These are the bells which still ring out today.

The most recent addition to the priory was the Kings Own Memorial Chapel. It was built in 1903 to commemorate the soldiers of the King's Own Border Regiment (Lancaster) who died fighting in the South African Wars.

4

Dalton Square

Lancaster's Dalton Square was first laid out during the Georgian era in 1783. The land was owned by John Dalton of Thurnham Hall. In common with all wealthy businessmen, he wanted to increase his family's wealth and so he split this land into building plots around a shared garden known as the Oval. His original idea was to produce an elegant square with grand, fashionable houses.

His dream was never realized as there was simply not enough wealth in the town to sustain this venture. By 1800 many of the plots had been broken up to provide housing that was much less grand and more affordable.

Dalton Square

The new town hall replaced Lancaster's earlier town hall which is still to be found in Market Square. The old building in Market Square is on the site of an ancient toll booth and was first built in 1668. It was later rebuilt in 1781. It is now Lancaster City Museum.

Lancaster corporation outgrew this building during the Victorian period but did not have the funds to relocate or build anew. The wealthy Lord Ashton again stamped his influence on the town and paid for the magnificent new Town Hall in Dalton Square. It was designed by E W Mountford who is also responsible for the Old Bailey in London. As with many of his buildings he used the world famous firm of Waring and Gillow as the main contractors for construction.

The Victoria Monument was originally intended for Williamson park but was included in the redesign of the oval. Queen Victoria and her four surrounding lions are sculpted from bronze. The four relief panels feature eminent Victorians from Richard Owen to Florence Nightingale. Lord Ashton also gives a nod to his father James Williamson Snr who appears on one of the reliefs.

The total cost of the town hall and the redesign of the gardens was £155,000. In conjunction with paying for the Ashton Memorial he spent a truly staggering sum. At today's costs this would equate to many millions of pounds.

Dalton Square

Dr Buck Ruxton

Dalton Square was the home of perhaps Lancaster's most infamous resident, Dr Buck Ruxton. Originally from Bombay his real name was Buktyar Rustomi. He took over a flourishing medical practice located at Number 2 Dalton Square in 1930. He lived at the practice with his wife, Isabella Kerr, their three children and their maid, Mary Rogerson.

Their relationship was known to be extremely tempestuous and often violent. He was a good looking man and liked the girls but Isabella was equally well liked and often socialized with Lancaster's elite. Ruxton had accused her on many occasions of having affairs.

One night in September 1935 he exploded in a violent rage, accusing Isabella of having a lover. He attacked her in the front room of the house and in his anger he strangled her to death. Unfortunately, the maid witnessed this event and Buck Ruxton killed her too.

The murder was made all the more infamous by his gruesome attempts to cover up his dreadful crime. He took the bodies upstairs to the bath where he drained them of their blood. He then dismembered their corpses and chopped them into many pieces before wrapping them in recent copies of local newspapers. The body parts of the two women were then driven to Scotland and thrown into a ravine.

The first body parts were found in Scotland on 29

September 1935 and were quickly followed by the discovery of more rotting body parts. There were so many pieces that the police originally thought they were dealing with several victims! The case is also famous in that it is one of the first where the prosecution used scientific techniques, such as fingerprinting and physical anthropology, in evidence.

Buck Ruxton was tried for murder in March 1936 and subsequently found guilty. Despite an appeal funded in part by the newspapers of the time paying for his story, he received the death penalty for his horrendous crime. He was hanged in Strangeways Prison, Manchester on 12 May 1936.

5

Lancaster Canal

The concept of the Lancaster canal was first raised in 1772. Unfortunately, the businessmen behind the venture could not agree a route and for over twenty years nothing was done other than making a few surveys of potential routes. It was not until 1791 when the country was in the grip of canal building mania that they were finally able to agree to build the canal, probably with some influence from Preston businessmen who had just missed out on being included on the Leeds and Liverpool Canal after its route was changed. It was conceived to transport coal from the Wigan and Bolton coalfields and limestone for agriculture

from Kendal. Hence its nickname, the Black and White Canal. It was also used to bring gunpowder from Kendal and was to link the towns of Preston, Lancaster and Kendal.

At the start of building, John Rennie was the chief engineer. He had earned a reputation as a builder of bridges although he is more notably the engineer responsible for the Bell Rock Lighthouse and London Bridge. His legacy remains to this day and many of the bridges on the canal are picturesque constructions and still in use today.

Work began in 1793 but it seems that indecision still plagued the developers and no southern connection had been decided upon. From Preston to Tewitfield, Lancaster canal

has no locks. It is a high contour canal following a line which is seventy feet above sea level. This first section was opened in 1797 but there was still no connection to the southern canal system.

Included in this section is the Lune Aqueduct one of the wonders of the waterways, designed by John Rennie himself and constructed by Alexander Stevens. It has five massive arches each with a span of more than seventy feet. Despite its solid construction the massive piers are sitting on timber piles. The aqueduct was built of stone with three feet of puddle clay lining to make it watertight. It took three years to build and cost staggering sum of £50,000.

Originally it was intended to build two aqueducts, one over the River Ribble at Preston and one over the River Lune in Lancaster. Only the Lancaster Aqueduct was ever built. The indecision over the southern connection and the huge cost of Lancaster Aqueduct, almost double the original estimate, meant that the canal company was unable to afford to build a crossing over the Ribble. That would need thirty two locks and an aqueduct costing more than £200,000. It was never built and a tramway was hastily agreed upon to link the southern end of the canal.

It was not until 1819 that the canal finally reached Kendal almost thirty years after construction had first begun. Coal

and lime were carried on the canal and despite its enormous cost and dubious southern tramway connection, a boom period followed for the company and all the towns linked by it. The final phase was a spur linking Glasson Dock at the head of the Lune Estuary in 1826, connecting the canal to the sea.

6

Williamson Park

Williamson's Park is built on a moorland site encompassing several former quarries from where Lancaster freestone was quarried during the eighteenth and nineteenth centuries. It is even possible that this site was quarried by the romans.

Lancaster freestone is a pale sandstone, which masons could cut and shape in any direction because it has no grain. It can be seen in many buildings in the centre of the town and was used in many of Lancaster's civic buildings.

The moor had been used informally for recreational purposes for many years but the original park was first laid

out by James Williamson I, the father of his more famous son Lord Ashton, during the early 1800s. He did this in order to create employment for his extensive mill workforce and the people of Lancaster in order to ease the extreme poverty caused by the Cotton Famine. The American Civil War was the main cause of this poverty. The American South tried to bring Britain into the war by placing a trade boycott on cotton,

later the Union placed a blockade on cotton exports making matters even worse. The effect in Lancaster was that many textile mills closed causing widespread poverty and much suffering. Building the park went some way to provide relief work for unemployed mill workers. Reflecting this hardship the top of the carriage drive was originally known as the Top of Hard Times it later became known as the Sixpence.

It was his son, James Williamson II who became Lord Ashton who furnished the park with its impressive monuments and buildings.

Lord Ashton gave the park to the Lancaster Corporation in 1881 with an endowment of £10,000. Lord Ashton continued to pay for many improvements most famously building the Ashton Memorial. He also paid for the erection of the Palm House, the fountain and a temple; all designed by Sir John Belcher. The temple is known locally as the pepperpot after its distinctive shape.

The Edwardian Palm House was opened just after the famous Ashton Memorial. It was designed by Sir John Belcher and was one of the improvements to the park implemented by Lord Ashton. It is now used as a butterfly house and tropical garden.

The Ashton Memorial

England's Grandest Folly

Williamson Park

Williamson Park is the home of England's largest and grandest folly, the Ashton Memorial. The monument stands at the highest point of Williamson Park and at 150 feet tall it dominates Lancaster's skyline. It is built from Portland stone, the favoured stone the Victorians used for their monumental buildings. The huge, grand staircase is built of Cornish granite and the great dome is clad in copper giving the memorial its striking green verdigris crown which can be seen for miles around.

This extravagant monument was designed by Sir John Belcher and built in the Edwardian Baroque style. Opened in 1909 it took nearly five years to build and cost £87,000. This was a truly staggering sum for a building designed ostensibly as a personal monument. It is hard to make comparison but today it would cost millions of pounds to build.

Lord Ashton's original motivation for building this huge folly was thought by local tradition to have been as a memorial to his second wife, Jessie Hume, but this is uncertain. When it was opened without ceremony it was simply dedicated to deceased relatives. It is known as The Ashton Memorial, and is perhaps fittingly, more of a monument to Lord Ashton himself.

There is public access the ground floor and the viewing balconies. On a clear day the views of Lancaster and the surrounding Lake District are stunning.

7

St Peter's Cathedral

In 1847 a plot of land known as Greenfield, was secured with the intent of building a church, a convent, a public cemetery and a school for the catholic community of Lancaster. The cemetery, school and convent where the first to be built completed by 1853 and land was left at the head of the plot for the building of a church when funds became available.

It was not until 1856 that money was bequeathed for the building of a church on this site by some of Lancaster's wealthy catholics. The church was designed by Edward Paley and is built in the gothic revival style. This is a deliberate

St Peter's Cathedral

architectural statement by Paley as its style mirrors English churches built in the 1300s when the Catholic Church was at its zenith in England. It is possibly Edward Paley's finest work. The foundation stone was laid on April 29, 1857 with great ceremony.

The divide between the catholic and protestant community during the 1800s is noticeably present in the building of this Church. One of the best builders in the town refused to undertake the masonry building work at his own price. His only reason for this refusal was upon 'religious grounds.'

Despite this the church rose rapidly from its foundations. The spire was finally topped with its cross in September 1859, less than three years after the foundation stone had been laid.

In 1879 the cathedral received its first peel of bells. These bells were later followed by the addition of two more bells giving St Peter's Cathedral a magnificent peel of ten bells which is something of a rarity for an English Roman Catholic church.

The cathedral is also unusual in that it is one of the few Roman Catholic churches in the country to contain images not only of King Herod but also of Henry VIII. Notably and extremely rarely for a catholic church there is also a depiction of Judas.

Located above the banks of the beautiful Lancaster canal St Peter's Cathedral is well worth a visit.

8

The Lune

Lancaster's rise as a port first began in the late 17th Century. As trade developed it included the transportation of slaves from Africa. Lancaster's merchants would sail to the west coast of Africa to pick up captured slaves, transport them to the plantations in the Caribbean and then bring exotic goods back to Lancaster. It is possible that the first ship to trade with the West Indies from Lancaster was the 'Lambe' which is known to have sailed in 1687 bringing mahogany, rum and cotton from Jamaica into the port.

Unfortunately, the River Lune at this time was not entirely

suitable for docking the increasing size and number of these merchant vessels. Nor was it organized to collect taxes properly. An Act of Parliament was passed to improve the navigability of the River Lune and to enable the enforcement of the payment of taxes on imported goods. This led to the building of St George's Quay in 1751.

The land for the first phase of the Quay was called the 'Summer Pasture' and was glebe land leased from the Vicar of St Mary's Priory. The Quay was built very quickly and relatively simply. A retaining wall was erected in the river and the land behind it was simply filled in. The land on the Quay

was then acquired by Lancaster's mercantile elite.

The 17th Century warehouses erected by these merchants are still with us today although most have now been converted into flats. They jostle for position and their higgledy-piggledy appearance now gives the quayside much of its charm. These warehouses are some of the finest Georgian buildings still surviving in England

The best of these is the Customs House. It was built in 1764 to the designs of Richard Gillow and was used for over 100 years. The house is built around a 'long room' as were many Georgian customs buildings. It mirrors the design

of the London Custom House built by Christopher Wren. It now houses Lancaster's maritime museum. The wealth generated from the port transformed the town's fortunes. Many of the first stone built buildings in Lancaster were built from this wealth and St George's Quay remains the most visible remnant of Lancaster's Georgian mercantile history.

There are several bridges crossing the River Lune in Lancaster. The most recent and unashamedly modern is the Millenium Bridge. This pedestrian bridge crosses the river roughly where a medieval bridge once stood.

The medieval bridge was bought by Brockbanks shipbuilders who took down one of the arches in order that they could sail fully masted ships from their shipyard at Green Ayre just a few hundred yards further up the river. They were able to do this because Lancaster had acquired Skerton bridge, a new bridge further upstream.

Skerton bridge was designed by Thomas Harrison, his first major commission. Harrison lived in Lancaster in the early 1780s and had studied in Italy. He is thought to have based his design for the bridge on a classical roman style bridge at

Rimini. The bridge was completed in September 1787 at a cost of £14,000.

It is notable as one of the first bridges in the country to use semi-elliptical arches which allow it to have a completely flat road deck and ballustrades along its entire length. The five original arches each span 65 feet. The bridge was also the first to contain storm water channels in the spaces between

the top of the arches and the road deck.

John Rennie came to see this bridge being built and there is an echo of Harrison's design in Rennie's Lune Aqueduct which for obvious reasons also required a flat carriageway. He must have been very impressed with this design because he also notably based his designs for the first Waterloo Bridge in London on Skerton Bridge - they were strikingly similar.

9

The Three Mariners

The Three Mariners is one of the oldest public houses in Lancaster possibly built as early as the 15th century. It is one of only two pubs in England to have a gravity fed cellar. The beer is kept on the first floor and fed down by gravity to the bar. This first floor cellar is also cooled by a natural spring running from castle rock.

As it stands today the pub looks to be oddly situated but you have to imagine it in its original context. It sits directly on Bridge Road which led down from Church Street to the medieval bridge. This would have been a narrow road built up on both sides. The old cobbles of this thoroughfare are

still to be seen outside the pub. Therefore in its heyday the Three Mariners would have sat at the heart of the port of Lancaster and on the busy main road down to the Quay and the warehouses that line it.

In fact, it is well known that sailors were press ganged from this pub during the 17th and 18th Centuries. Lancaster at this time was a thriving merchant port which meant that experienced able bodied seamen could be found in the port's drinking houses. The Royal Navy would have had no qualms about impressing these experienced sailors in time of war.

There are many stories of ghosts and haunting. There are reports through the years of a blonde lady being seen in the cellar and things have been said to be thrown around. How much of this activity can be attributed to the spirits consumed by enthusiastic revellers is still open to debate.

10

Epilogue

For such a small town Lancaster has a wealth of history rivalling some of the larger cities in England and it must be remembered that Lancaster's population for much of its history was less than ten thousand people.

Many of the oldest surviving buildings were built from the wealth generated by the merchant classes of the Georgian era but evidence of older roman and medieval phases still survives under this modern framework. The canal corridor was for hundreds of years lined with many huge mills some of which still survive having been converted and beautified into businesses and residences.

Epilogue

But Lancaster was indeed a mill town filled with the dark satanic mills and chimneys of the 18th and 19th Centuries. Williamson's Bath Mill was still in working into the early 1970s. Bath Mill was so huge its site was large enough to enable a substantial housing estate to be built upon it.

The impact of Lancaster's historical development is still readily visible encompassing many of the great events from our national history. The castle remains, despite extensive historical alterations and uses over its thousand year development. The great canal building boom and the mills of the 17th and 18th Centuries have left very visible marks on the city.

Lancaster has been visibly transformed over the centuries by all of its changing fortunes and new industries. Lancaster has much to offer and the visitor only has to gently scratch the surface of this historic city to be rewarded with a rich history stretching back over a thousand years.